Leaves fall just before Halloween

Halloween

Valerie Bodden

Creative Education

Published by Creative Education

123 South Broad Street, Mankato, Minnesota 56001

Creative Education is an imprint of The Creative Company

Designed by Rita Marshall

Photographs by Roy Gumpel

Cover illustration © 1996 Roberto Innocenti

Copyright © 2006 Creative Education

International copyright reserved in all countries. No part of this book may be reproduced in any form without written permission from the publisher.

Printed in the United States of America

Library of Congress Cataloging-in-Publication Data

Bodden, Valerie. Halloween / by Valerie Bodden.

p. cm. — (My first look at holidays)

ISBN 1-58341-368-5

1. Halloween—Juvenile literature. I. Title.

GT4965.B64 2005   394.2646—dc22   2004057095

First edition 9 8 7 6 5 4 3 2 1

Halloween

All Hallow's Eve 6

Trick-or-Treat 8

Halloween Decorations 14

Scary Fun 18

Hands-On: Paper Pumpkins 22

Additional Information 24

All Hallow's Eve

Halloween is an old **holiday**. It began more than 2,000 years ago. People celebrate Halloween on October 31.

Long ago, Halloween had a different name. It was called All Hallow's Eve. People celebrated the **harvest** on All Hallow's Eve. They ate a lot of food and danced. Some people lit big fires outside.

HALLOWEEN FUN USUALLY BEGINS AT SUNSET

Some people thought ghosts and witches came out on All Hallow's Eve. So they wore ghost and witch **costumes** to protect themselves. Then the real ghosts and witches could not tell the difference.

Trick-or-Treat

Today, many kids go trick-or-treating on Halloween. They wear costumes. Some kids dress like ghosts or witches. Some dress like clowns. Others try to look like their favorite cartoon character.

People in England and Ireland used to make jack-o'-lanterns out of turnips.

MANY PEOPLE MAKE JACK-O'-LANTERNS AT HALLOWEEN

MANY PEOPLE DRESS UP AS GHOSTS

Trick-or-treaters ring doorbells and say "Trick or treat!" People may give them candy or other treats.

Kids used to play tricks on people who did not give them treats. That is why they said "Trick or treat!" Today, most kids do not play tricks. But they still say "Trick or treat!"

In Scotland,
trick-or-treaters have to
tell a story or sing a song
to get candy.

A BOY IN A ONE-EYED PIRATE COSTUME

Trick-or-treaters carry bags or pails to hold all of their candy. They say "Thank you!" to the people who give them treats.

Halloween Decorations

Many people decorate for Halloween. Orange and black are Halloween colors. Ghosts and bats are favorite Halloween decorations. So are fake spider webs. Some people hang **skeletons** from trees.

The largest pumpkin ever grown weighed more than 1,300 pounds (585 kg)!

CHOOSING THE PERFECT PUMPKIN IS PART OF THE HALLOWEEN FUN

Pumpkins are Halloween decorations, too. They come in all shapes and sizes. Most are orange. But some are yellow or even white.

Many people **carve** jack-o'-lanterns. First, they cut a pumpkin open. They scoop out the seeds. Then, they carve a face into the pumpkin. They put a candle in the pumpkin to make it glow.

Jack-o'-lanterns can be funny or scary

Scary Fun

Some people have parties on Halloween. They tell ghost stories. They may give prizes to the people with the best costumes.

Bobbing for apples is a fun Halloween game. People try to pull an apple out of a tub of water with their teeth!

Some people make their own costumes

Some people go to haunted houses on Halloween. Haunted houses are dark. They are full of scary noises. Witches laugh. Wolves howl. Floors creak. People dressed as monsters jump out and say "Boo!"

Halloween can be scary and fun. Wear a costume! Play some games! Enjoy your candy! Make a jack-o'-lantern or two to set out for Halloween.

In Mexico, people celebrate the Day of the Dead instead of Halloween.

TRICK-OR-TREATING AND PARTIES MAKE HALLOWEEN FUN

Hands-on: Paper Pumpkins

Make a string of jack-o'-lanterns for Halloween.

What You Need

Orange paper
Crayons
Scissors
A long piece of green yarn
Clothespins

What You Do

1. Draw several pumpkins as big as your hand on the orange paper. Make sure to draw a long stem on the top of each one.
2. Have a grown-up help you cut out the pumpkins.
3. Use a black crayon to draw eyes, a nose, and a mouth on each pumpkin. Color the stems green.
4. Clip the pumpkins to the yarn with clothespins. Now hang up your string of jack-o'-lanterns!

MAKING MASKS IS AS FUN AS WEARING THEM

Index

All Hallow's Eve 6, 8
costumes 8, 18, 20
decorations 14, 16
ghosts 8, 14
haunted houses 20
jack-o'-lanterns 9, 16, 20, 22
parties 18
pumpkins 15, 16
trick-or-treating 8, 12, 13, 14

Words to Know

carve—cut something into a shape
costumes—special clothes that make people look like someone or something else
harvest—the plants that are picked from farmers' fields
holiday—a special day that happens every year
skeletons—the bones that make up a person's body

Read More

Haugen, Brenda. *Halloween*. Minneapolis, Minn.: Picture Window Books, 2004.

Klingel, Cynthia, and Robert B. Noyed. *Halloween*. Chanhassen, Minn.: The Child's World, 2003.

Rosinsky, Natalie M. *Halloween*. Minneapolis, Minn.: Compass Point Books, 2003.

Explore the Web

Animated Halloween http://www.animatedhalloween.com
BlackDog's Halloween Party http://www.blackdog.net/holiday/halloween
HalloweenKids.com http://www.halloweenkids.com